Where is Noah?

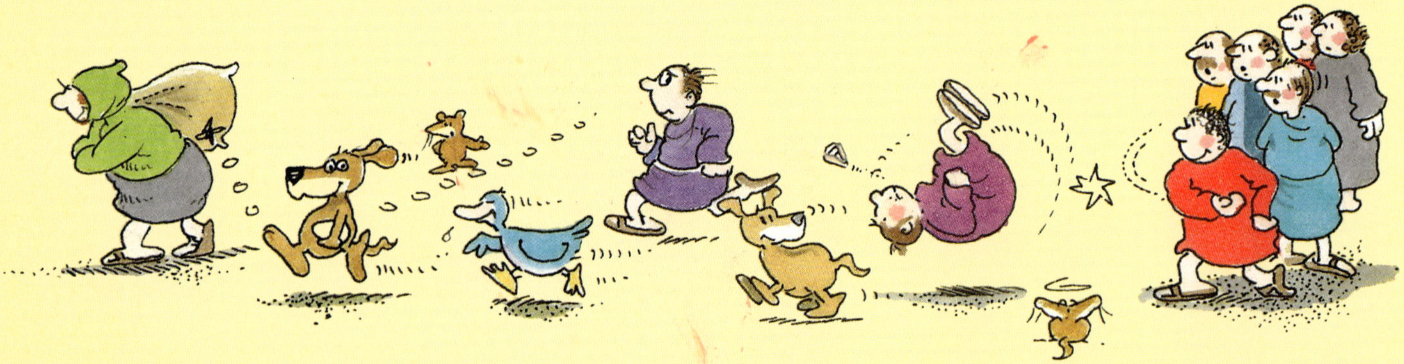

A Where-in-the-Bible adventure book

Where is Noah?

RHONA PIPE
Illustrated by Chris Masters

HUNT & THORPE

Where is Noah? And his wife?
Noah loved God all his life.
On the rooftop loud and clear
They preached—did many stay to hear?

No. We're very sad to say,
People were bad in Noah's day.

❓ Can you see Noah preaching and his wife praying?

God said,
"Build a boat, and make it strong,
Make it tall and very long.
Have three decks and rooms galore."

"Whoops!" said Noah. "Where's my saw?"

❓ *Can you find Noah's saw, axe and hammer?*

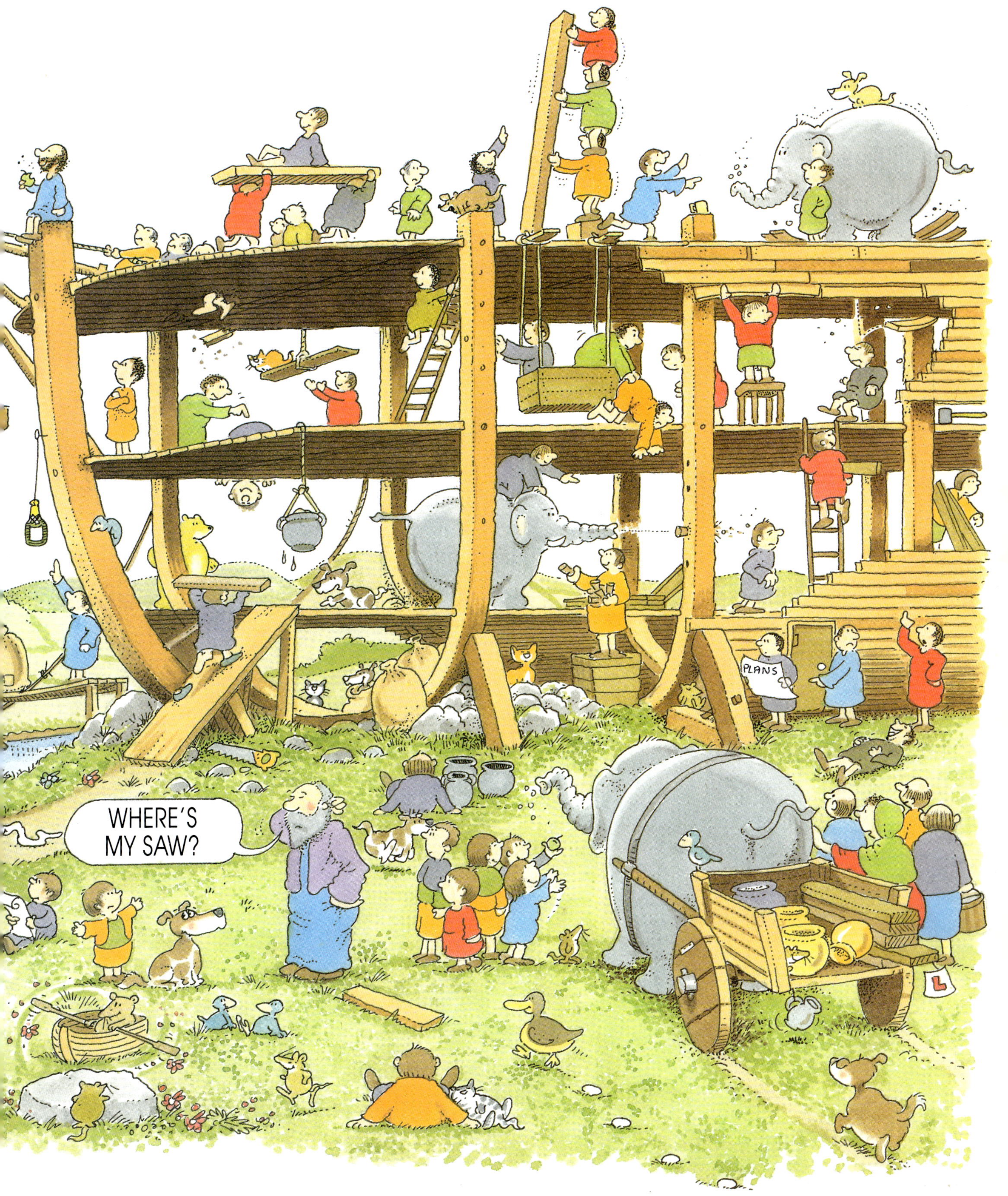
WHERE'S MY SAW?
PLANS

The people said,
"Noah's such a featherbrain.
Why, we've never even seen it rain!"

He had three sons, Japheth, Ham and Shem.
Can you spot the three of them?

❓ *Find Noah's three sons and their wives.*
(Clue: Their wives have packed their suitcases.
Each son is marked with the first letter of his name.)

God said,
"Get seven pairs of every kind
Of bird and beast that you can find.
And lots of food, put that on too."

There are bananas for—guess who?

? Where are the fourteen bananas and two monkeys?

All inside? God shut the door.
Then the rain began to pour.
The rain came down, the water rose—

? *Can you see the elephant's nose?*

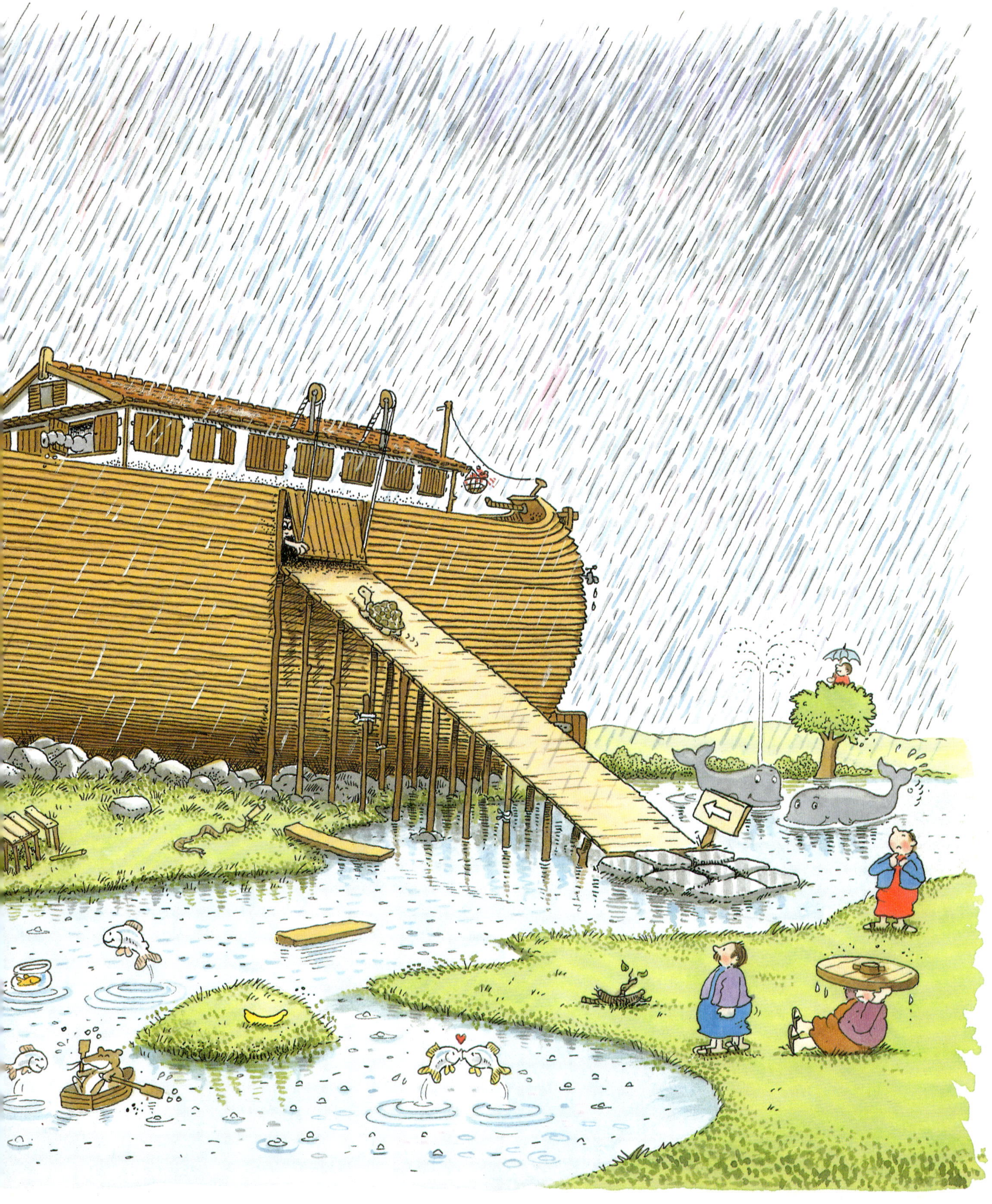

But God did not forget his friend.
One day the rain came to an end.
Rippling water round the ark—

❓ *Can you spot the whales and sharks?*

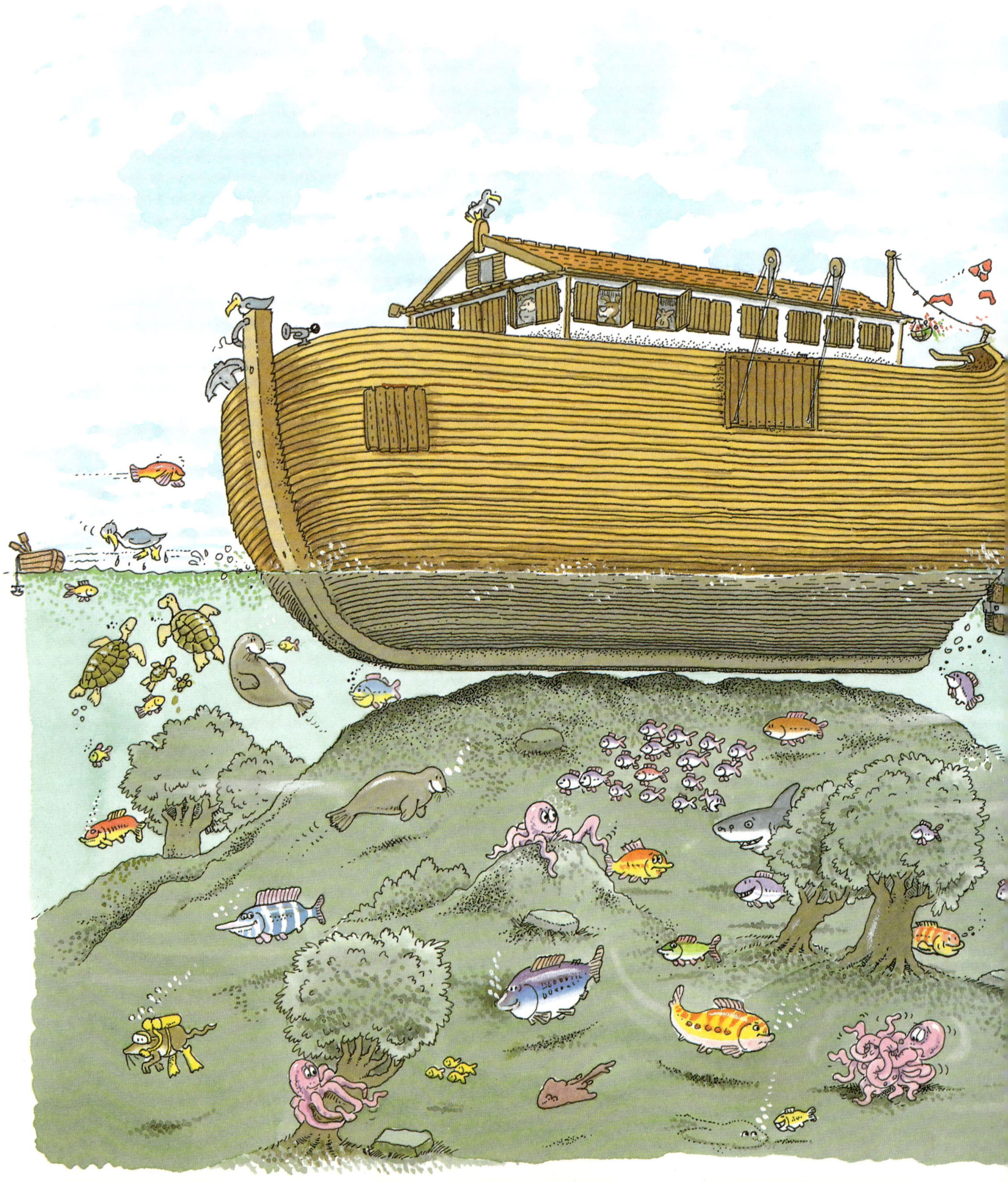

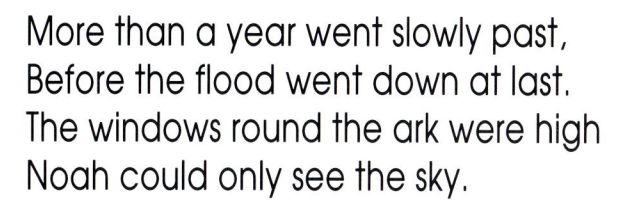

More than a year went slowly past,
Before the flood went down at last.
The windows round the ark were high
Noah could only see the sky.

Was there any land about?
The gentle dove went to find out.

❓ *The dove found some trees. Can you find her?*

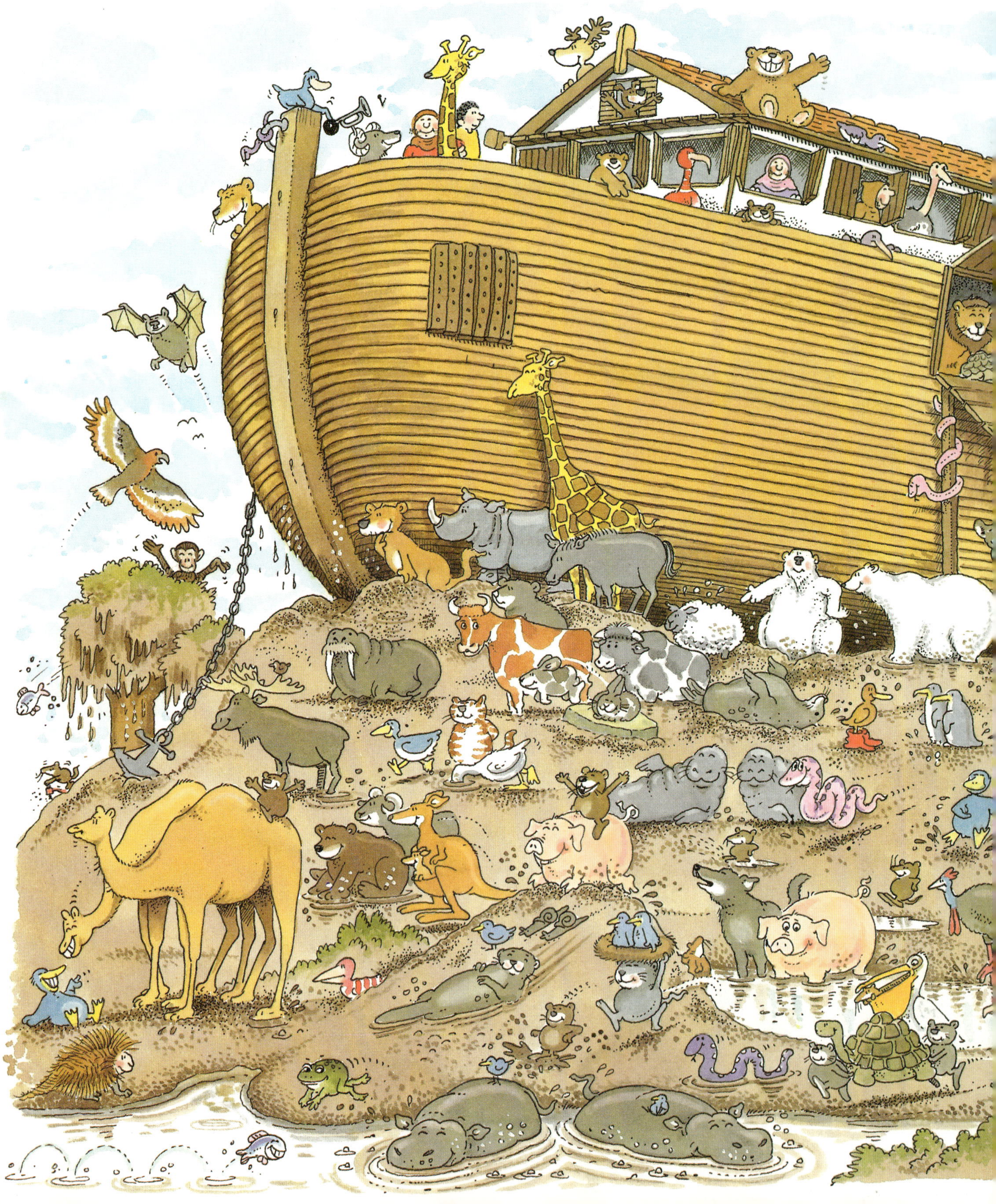

Off with the roof— now look around,
Thick brown mud on all the ground.
Glorious mud, hip, hip, hurray!

Find five baby lambs as they play.

? *Where did the monkey go?*

God said,
"I won't destroy the earth again.
Seasons will change until time ends.
The rainbow in the sky above
Is the sign to show my love."

? *Has everybody left the boat?*
Where's the silly billy goat?

THANK YOU, GOD.

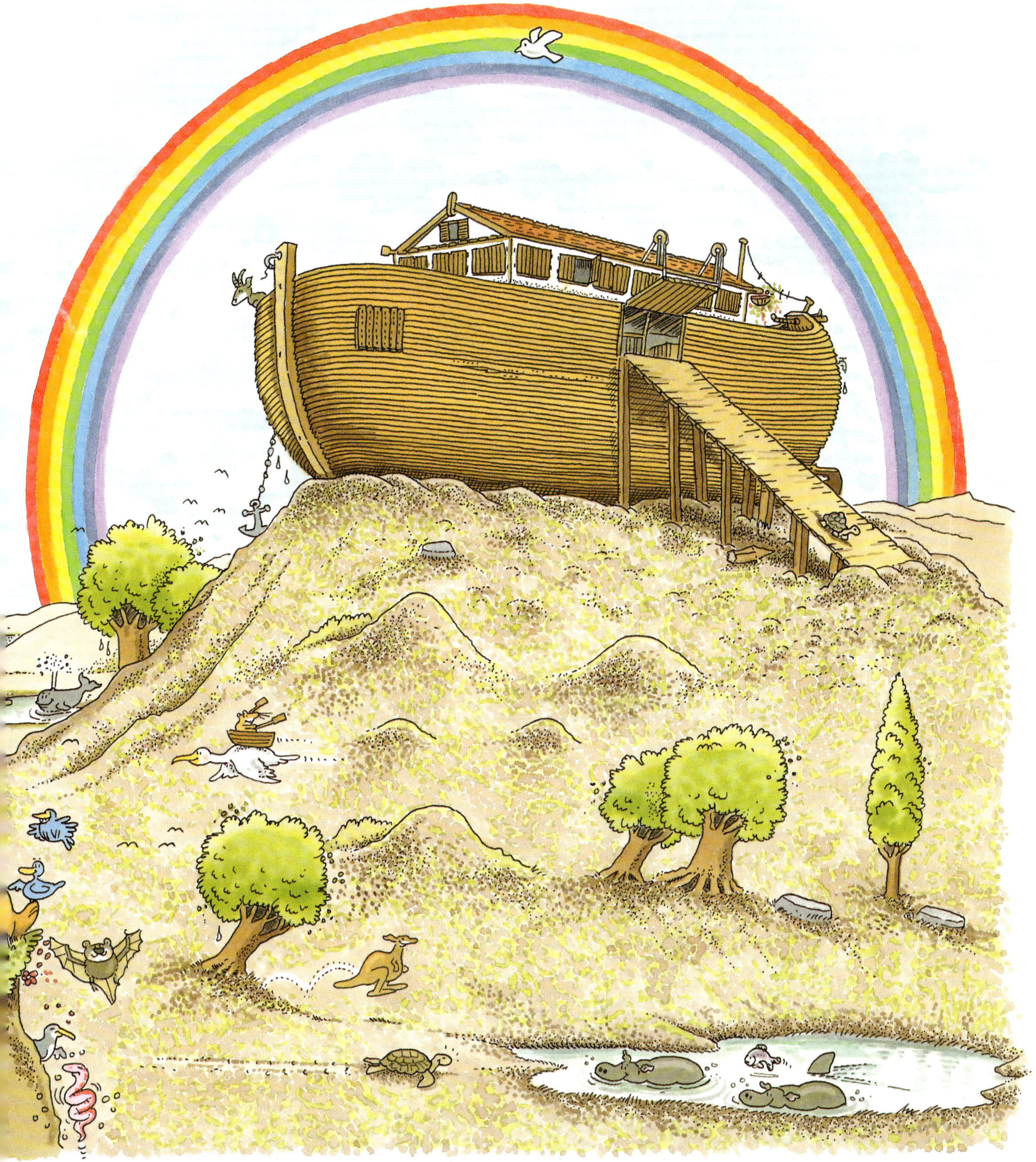

Copyright © 1993 Hunt & Thorpe
Text © 1993 by Rhona Pipe
Illustrations © 1993 by Chris Masters
Originally published by Hunt & Thorpe in hardback 1993
This edition published 1997
Reprinted 2000

ISBN 1 85608 322 5

All rights reserved. Except for
brief quotations in critical articles or reviews,
no part of this book may be reproduced in any manner
without prior written permission from the publishers. Write to:
John Hunt Publishing Ltd., 46a West Street,
Alresford, Hants SO24 9AU, UK

A CIP catalogue record for the book
is available from the British Library.

Manufactured in Singapore.

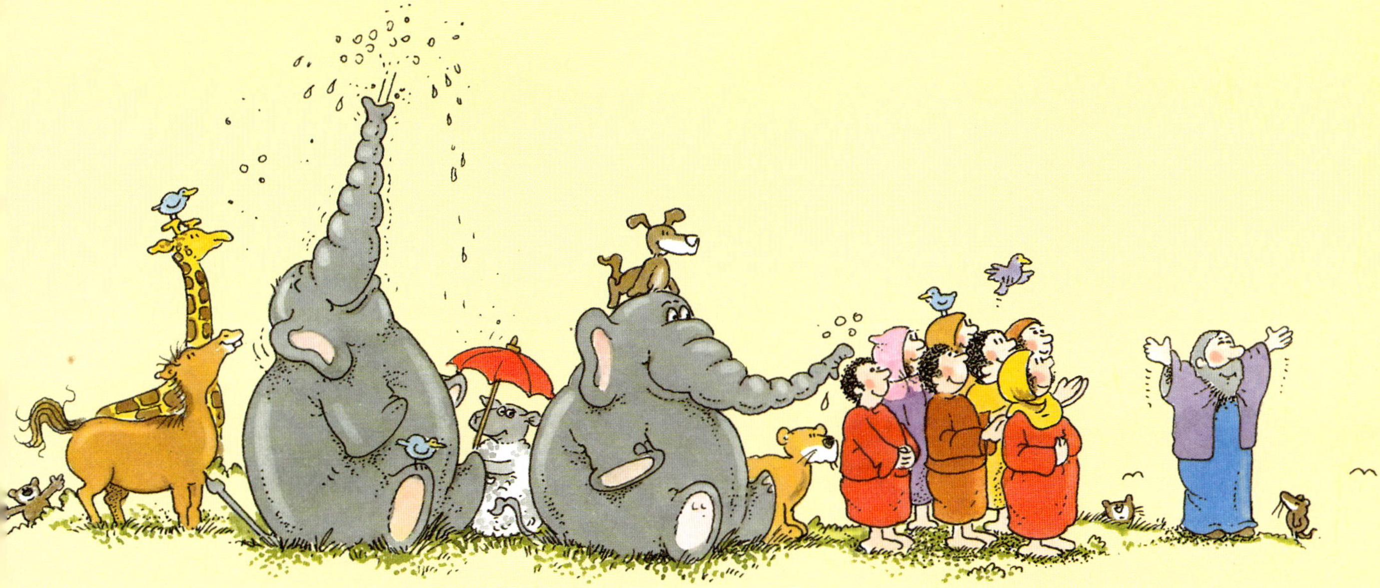